LIFe'S STILL THE PITS

First published in Great Britain in 1999 by

Chameleon Books

76 Dean Street

London W1V 5HA

Copyright for text © Generation Publications

CIP data for this title is available from the British Library

ISBN 0 233 99499 8

Book and jacket Design Generation Studio.

Reprographics by Jade Reprographics

Printed in Spain.

ACKNOWLEDGEMENTS:

A special thanks to Dave Crowe, Mark Peacock, Eddie Schillace, Joe Crowe, Tim Vigon, Linda Baritski, Paul Sudbury, (Veronica, Becky, Ellie & Ben), Matthew Sudbury, John Delaney, Terry Maxwell.

PHOTOGRAPH ACKNOWLEDGEMENTS:

All photographs courtesy of Allsports.

DEDICATED TO:

**Mary Killingworth
the woman whose driving is still
'The Pits'**

"Women drivers take a lot of stick - most of it undeserved - so I am glad that this book exists to remind women road users everywhere that when it comes to the 'crunch' there's more egg (fried, scrambled, poached and just plain hard-boiled) on men's faces than on women's. My own achievements on the road may be deemed humble, but perhaps some of the drivers that appear in the pages that follow should have taken a leaf out of my book and stuck on the hard shoulder rather than mixing in it the fast lane."

Maureen Rees (from BBC1's Driving School)

Damon, try saying "Vroom, vroom."

World Chump

Damon Hill made an inauspicious start to his short career at the Arrows team in 1997. The cars set off on the warm up lap prior to the start of the season opening Australian Grand Prix, unfortunately one of them did not make it back to the grid. Hill's new car broke down, leaving the reigning champion stranded.

As they say money doesn't always guarantee style.

Hill Throttled

Damon Hill's finest moment in the Arrows undoubtedly came at the Hungarian Grand Prix when he led into the final lap, having even pulled off a brilliant overtaking manoeuvre on old rival Michael Schumacher. A throttle problem on the last lap, however, meant Hill was passed by Villeneuve in the Williams and had to settle for second place.

Schu Ceases To Exist

Jacques Villeneuve clinched the 1997 Drivers Championship at Jerez in Spain, despite the best, and worst efforts of Michael Schumacher. As the pair duelled for the title on the track, Schumacher's Ferrari developed a problem, and as Villeneuve attempted to overtake, Schuey clearly tried to run the pair of them off the road. He failed, Villeneuve won, and Schumacher was retrospectively wiped from the 97 Championship.

Bernie Bargain

F1 Chief Bernie Ecclestone landed in hot water in 1997 when it turned out he had made a £1m donation to the Labour party, and not long after, the Labour Government announced a moratorium on the banning of tobacco sponsorship in F1 racing. Were the two connected? Who knows, but Bernie got his money back from the Party, as well as some nice coverage in the media.

Q. What is the similarity between Mika Hakkinen and a sperm?

A. They both stand a 1 in 4 million chance of becoming a human

Expelled To Excel

In an interview with Total Sport magazine, Jacques Villeneuve stated that the best thing that ever happened to him was: "Being kicked out of school, because I started racing."

Battle of the fags.

Long Drive

Frenchman Pierre Levegh almost caused a sensation in the 1952 Le Mans 24 hour race when he attempted to become the first man to drive the entire race single-handedly. He nearly did it, too. It wasn't until the 23rd hour that the tired 46-year-old, who was leading at the time, missed a gear change which badly damaged the engine of his Talbot-Lago, forcing him to retire.

It's the only chequered flag you're going to get this season.

Ferrari are glad to see the back of them.

Le Mans Tragedy

Despite failing in his solo attempt to win Le Mans Pierre Levegh did, however, go into the Le Mans history books, for a much more sombre reason. In 1955 he raced for the Mercedes team. Just two hours into the race Levegh's Mercedes caught Lance Macklin's Austin Healey with disastrous consequences. The Mercedes left the track and exploded, killing the driver instantly. The engine and debris flew into the crowd and over 80 spectators lost their lives - the worst ever tragedy in the history of motor sport.

I wonder why Formula one attracts so many women?

They look tyred out.

Racing Stars

Top movie stars have been attracted to the glamour of motor racing, most famously Steve McQueen and Paul Newman. In 1971 McQueen drove in the Sebring 12 Hours race in Florida, partnering American driver Peter Revson in a Porsche. McQueen finished second, beaten only by Mario Andretti.

Paul Newman entered Le Mans as a driver in 1979 and helped steer his Porsche to second place. Newman was beaten by a German driver Klaus Ludwig who was helped by two American brothers, who the FBI subsequently discovered to be drug barons.

F-1 magazine asked Ralph Schumacher if women made good drivers:
"Some are, some aren't. But sometimes they can be a bit too patient," replied Schumacher Junior.

"You meet a much nicer class of person at the back of the grid." Graham Hill. "Dad once told me you meet a better class of people at the back of the grid, but I'm not so sure." Damon Hill

False Starting

The 1969 Le Mans race was the last to feature the running start when drivers sprinted across the track, jumped into their cars and raced off. By 1969 the prevailing opinion was that such a start was dangerous, and Belgian driver Jacky Ickx made his own protest at the start of the race by simply strolling across to his car and pulling away from the grid in last place. Just a few minutes later, British driver John Woolfe was killed after crashing his Porsche - he had failed to secure his seatbelts properly at the start.

"Apparently he's just lost his green hair dye."

"Ha, Ha! I spit in ze face of.....shit, I can't see."

There's Confidence For You

In the 1996 Portuguese Grand Prix, Jacques Villeneuve pulled an audacious overtaking move on Michael Schumacher. Afterwards he said: "It was fun overtaking on the outside of the turn. I told the team before the race that I thought we could do it, they said they would come and pick me out of the guard rail."

Ferrari Boobs

Ferrari the car maker lost a legal battle with Ferrari the porn star to try and force Lola Ferrari, real name Eve Valois, to change her name again, saying it was "destroying their image."

Ferrari the porn star, who has had some 18 breast enlargement operations, won the case, with the judge turning against Ferrari the car maker, saying: "She is well known as Lola Ferrari in her own right and people do not get her confused with Italian sports cars." Apart, perhaps, from those featuring twin air bags.

"He says either the car is stationary, or it's on the move!"

Master Driver

Ayrton Senna recorded an amazing 65 pole positions in his Formula 1 career, achieving first place on the grid in over 40% of his races.

Young Bruce

When Bruce McLaren won the 1959 US Grand Prix he was just 22 years old, and the youngest driver ever to win a race in Formula 1 history. He still is.

Fat Nige

When Nigel Mansell returned to Formula 1 in 1995, it was at the behest (and funds) of McLaren. Either someone measured him up wrong or Mansell put on weight, because the cockpit of his new car was too narrow for the ex-world champion to fit in to. Mansell therefore missed the first two races of the season while modifications were made, but when he finally did climb into the McLaren he quickly declared it useless and quit the team.

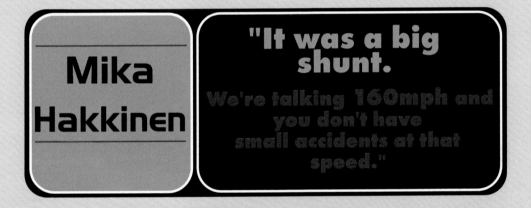

Mika Hakkinen

"It was a big shunt. We're talking 160mph and you don't have small accidents at that speed."

Not A Good Bet

Controversy for Formula 1 at the 1998 Australian Grand Prix. With the McLarens of David Coulthard and Mika Hakkinen dominant all weekend, it looked odds on with three laps to go that Coulthard would lead his team-mate home in a McLaren-Mercedes one-two. Alas for those who had placed a bet on the Scot, that's not what transpired. In an apparent pre-race agreement, Coulthard slowed down to let Hakkinen take first place on the podium. But this is racing we're talking about here isn't it?

Any suggestion that Fisichella is a good driver is groundless.

The Life Of Brian

In the days before he was driving a dominant car, Mika Hakkinen used to rely on a plastic turtle called Brian to bring him luck. Brian was always around when Hakkinen raced, but unfortunately Hakkinen never won. Adding two and two together, the McLaren pit crew kidnapped Brian, took him out the back of the pit-lane, poured petrol on the hapless toy and set fire to him. Hakkinen won his first GP soon after, at Jerez in 1997.

Getting Shirty

Some 8,000 T-shirts proclaiming "Michael Schumacher World Champion 1997" had to be destroyed after Jacques Villeneuve took the title from under the German's nose.

Sure you can have your cake and eat it.

"Just 1 lap to go?"

> **"You win some, you lose some, you wreck some."**
>
> Dale Erhardt

Weight Problem

1998 did not get off to a good start for Damon Hill and the Jordan team. After finishing a creditable 10th at Brazil, Hill was disqualified for his car being underweight. "I don't think it gets much worse than this," said team boss Eddie Jordan. Maybe not, but his team still had to wait until July and the British Grand Prix before scoring its first point of the season, thanks not to Hill but to Ralph Schumacher.

Jacques trying to
re-adjust his
revolutionary
new hair piece.

Wacky Winners

Research published in the *Daily Mail* figured that if the cartoon series Wacky Races had been run according to Formula 1 rules, the Slag Brothers would have triumphed with four wins in the 34 races, plus a host of other podium finishes.

"When Ferrari Leggo me I still have a drive. Ha, ha!"

"Hello, Damon, new in the pit crew, but give me a shout if you need anything... petrol, tyres with a spot of air in, ...that sort of stuff...."

Unbelievable. I'm really Murray Walker?
Unbelievable."

Monza's Mourning

Italy's Monza circuit, the spiritual home of Ferrari, has also been the scene of some of racing's worst tragedies. Emilio Materassi, in 1928, crashed on the pit straight, killing himself and 28 spectators, and in 1931, three more spectators died when Phillipe Etancelin crashed, although he survived. Ferrari's own Wolfgang von Trips died in the 1961 Italian Grand prix, and 14 members of the crowd were also killed after von Trips collided with British driver Jim Clark.

See, blondes really do have fun.

Rothm
Williams R

TESCO

"Right, lads, nick what you can and be back here in 5 minutes."

Tree Trouble

In the 1985 World Sportscar Championship, a race had to be stopped when a tree fell across the track of the famous Monza circuit.

"I'll retire sooner rather than later. I don't want to be like **Mansell**."
Michael Schumacher.

"I think I will climb **Everest**, just as long as there is a nice bar at the top."
Gerhard Berger's plans on his retirement.

Take It Out Of His Wages

Colin McRae's repair bill for his Subaru through the 1996 season topped over £1 million. Team manager David Richards was not amused: "It's not unfortunate. It's incompetent."

Hit In The Wallet

Rally driver Colin McRae managed to plough into a group of spectators at a service area during the 1996 Argentinian rally, a feat which earned him a fine of £166,000. After the fine was announced McRae said: "The result of the hearing hasn't been all bad. It just means the Christmas presents will be smaller this year."

Brave Johnny

Johnny Herbert was lucky to survive a crash at Brands Hatch in a Formula 3000 race in 1988. The pile-up involved 18 cars in total, and Herbert's description of his injuries was: "the left ankle was near enough ripped off, the right one was smashed and deformed." The surgeon said he'd never race again, but Herbert was back driving go-karts within four months, although he had to be lifted from wheelchair to cockpit to compete. Within seven months he was making his Formula 1 debut in Brazil, where he steered his Benetton home in fourth place.

Havoc In The Rain

In the 1975 British Grand Prix at Silverstone, a severe downpour on lap 55 caused mayhem among the cars, and most spun off the track. In fact, when the race was stopped because of the weather, only four cars remained on the circuit, led by Emerson Fittipaldi. The result of the race was decided on the lap preceding the rain, so four of the top five places were given to drivers who had crashed by the time the race was actually called to a halt.

50 Up At Silverstone

Motor racing first took place at Silverstone in 1948. The first ever World Championship race was held there in 1950, and among the spectators was King George VI.

If only he could find his
first gear quicker.

"Some people's response is: 'We don't have the money to develop the system.' It's more accurate to say they don't have the brains."

Ron Dennis

fires at those griping at McLaren's technical dominance at the start of 1998.

"I am very pleased to be only **two and half seconds** off the pace."

Damon Hill

in praise of his Arrows car.

"We're going to throw the book at you pal - no tax and bald tyres for starters.

"In my sport the quick are too often **listed among the dead.**" Jackie Stewart

Air Jordan

Martin Brundle made a spectacular start to the 1996 Grand Prix season. Lap one of the first race in Australia saw Brundle's Jordan leap into the air, somersault over a couple of other cars, and land upside down in the gravel trap. Brundle emerged unscathed and ran back to the pits to claim the spare car to join the race re-start. Lap two of the re-started race saw Brundle approach the same corner with no apparent trepidation, but he got out of shape and slid off into the same gravel trap. This time his race was finished.

Graham Hill

"Grand Prix racing is like balancing an egg on a spoon while shooting the rapids."

"So after first gear I put it in second?"

"What an incredible lap that must have been. I would have loved to have seen it." **Damon Hill** throws in a scorching qualifying lap in an Arrows, the TV producer missed it, and Martin Brundle laments.

"Aerodynamics, aerodynamics and aerodynamics. That's what matters here." Eddie Irvine's view of Hockenheim.

"I try to keep my bra on at all times." Georgie Hill on how she avoids causing a stir in the pit lane after Jean Alesi's girlfriend was banned.

"Just tell her I had a flat tyre and I'll be back soon."

Mind Lapse

The 1998 season was not a happy one for Johnny Herbert in his Sauber. Herbert found his status as lead man usurped with the arrival of Jean Alesi, and the ignominy was increased by Herbert's performance at the British Grand Prix. They say the first person you should beat is your team-mate, and at Silverstone Herbert led Alesi by a whisker until the team used the radio to tell him to let Alesi through. Herbert slowed, waved the Frenchman through, and promptly slid off the circuit, hitting the grass backwards.

Herbert said later: "I wasn't paying attention to what I was doing."

"'Cuse me, mate, is this the audition for 'London's Burning'?"

"Amazing. S...
son. Do y...

What The...?

Michael Schumacher's win at the British Grand Prix in 1998 was marred by controversy and confusion. Approaching the chequered flag, Schumacher stunned all by whipping his Ferrari down the pit lane to take a stop-go penalty. Commentators and spectators alike therefore saw Mika Hakkinen's McLaren cross the line first, but were later told that Schuey had crossed the line in the pit lane and was therefore the winner. As for the stop-go penalty, it was later described as a mistake. Nothing like a clear-cut, uncomplicated ending then...

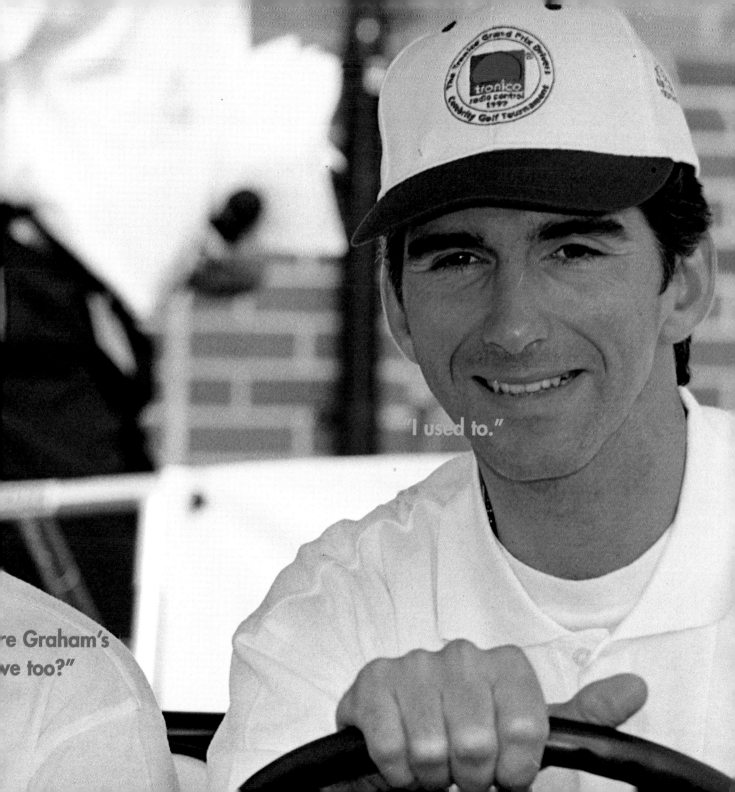

"I used to."

re Graham's
ve too?"

Temper Temper

Mika Salo had a spot of taxi trouble while back home in Helsinki. Salo jumped a queue for cabs outside a nightclub, but was ordered out of the car by the taxi driver. Salo then proceeded to aim a hefty kick or two at the cab door, causing some £2000 worth of damage. At least he paid for the damage later.

Mario Andretti

"You always see gaps in racing. The trick is to make sure that they are wider than your car."

"I'm not there just to go for a Sunday afternoon drive."
Alexander Wurz
on his preparations
for a GP.

Free Floor

McLaren boss Ron Dennis splashed out on a new floor for the team garage at the British Grand Prix. He had a marble floor put down, instead of the usual paint. He later explained: "We're spending £1 million on tiles in the new factory, so I asked the suppliers for a few more - they're free!"

No Bull

Sauber's woes for 1998 were added to from a rather unexpected direction at the Canadian and French Grand Prix. The team's title sponsor is Red Bull, an energy replenishing drink. Unfortunately it is not yet licensed in France or Canada, so it was therefore unavailable in the team motorhome. Just water, chaps...

Michael's 'Love Machine' going
for pole position.

Fags R us.

Alexander Wurz managed to go airborne in Canada in his Benetton, flipped it over and skated upside down into the gravel pit. The young Austrian jumped out of the wreckage, and told his team to prepare the spare car while he nipped to the loo. In the restarted race he drove through from 16th to finish fourth and in the points.

"My first priority **is to finish above rather than** below **the ground."**

James Hunt

Jos Back On Track

Jos Verstappen stepped back into Formula 1 at the French Grand Prix, replacing Jan Magnussen at Stewart. Not a great start for Verstappen's revived career, though, he stalled the Stewart-Ford on the grid at the start and forced the race to be set off again.

On Yer Bike

Austrian sensation Alexander Wurz already has a taste for world championship victories. At the age of 12 he was the world's best at BMX biking.

Try Changing Gear

David Coulthard was taken by surprise at the restart of the 1998 French Grand Prix as Villeneuve, Schumacher and Irvine all roared away from his McLaren. "I don't understand it," said the Scot afterwards. "I thought I made an OK start. I've never seen three cars disappear like that in my life. The two Ferraris and Villeneuve: zoom, zoom, zoom. I'll never recover from that. I'm emotionally scarred for life!"

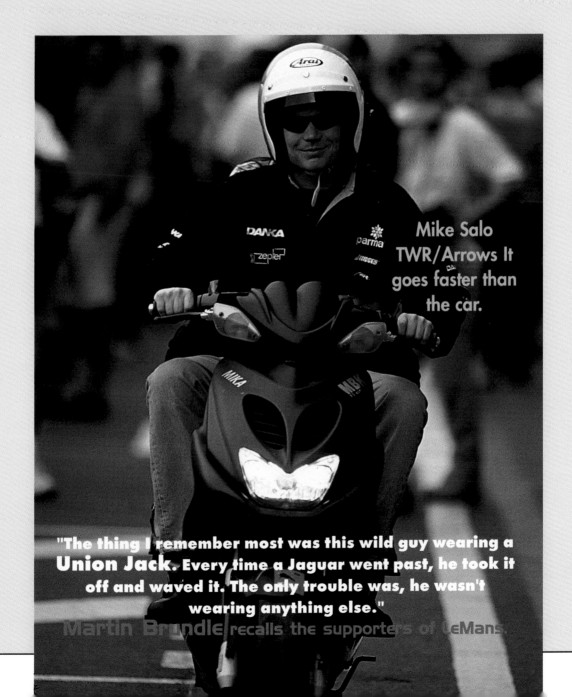

Mike Salo
TWR/Arrows It
goes faster than
the car.

"The thing I remember most was this wild guy wearing a **Union Jack**. Every time a Jaguar went past, he took it off and waved it. The only trouble was, he wasn't wearing anything else."

Martin Brundle recalls the supporters of LeMans.

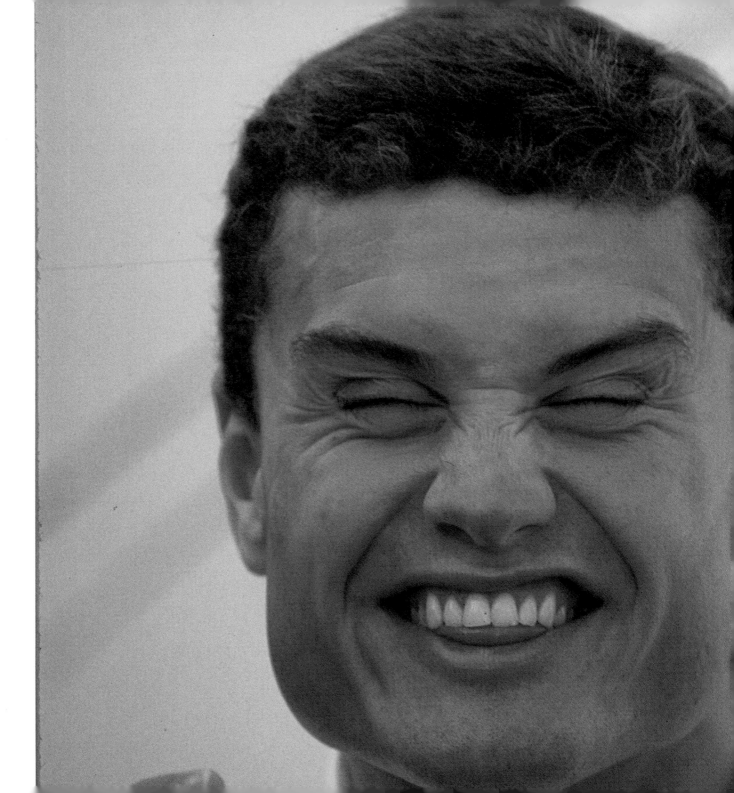

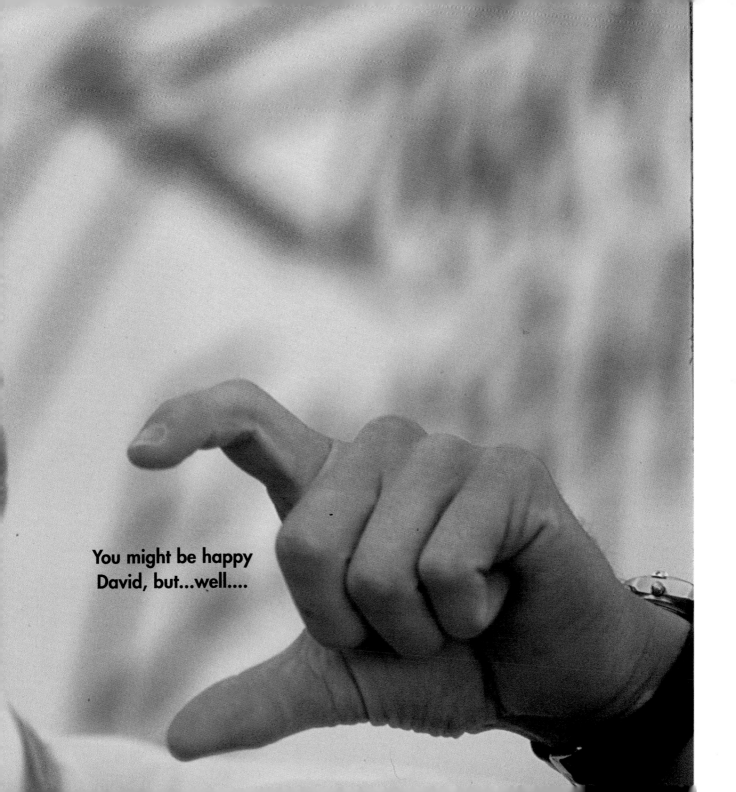

You might be happy
David, but...well....

A Bernie Ecclestone shareholders meeting.

On The Cheap

The Minardi team, perpetual minnows of the Grand Prix circus, operate on a total annual budget of around £20 million. Approximately half size of the retainer that Michael Schumacher receives from Ferrari.

Giancarlo
Fisichella
Jordon Peugeot
Tyre blow out at
200 mph.
Wooss!

Good Work In The Pits

The world's first ever Grand Prix was held in 1906 and was won by Hungarian Ferene Sziz in a Renault. Sziz won the 770 mile race (run over two days) by half an hour. Part of his success was due to the swiftness of his pit stops. His Renault team managed to complete a tyre change in a startlingly quick four minutes - some 11 minutes faster than the norm at the time.

Champagne Bernie

Champagne makers Moët & Chandon pulled the plug on their sponsorship of Formula 1 at the end of 1997. After all, £100,000 a race just to see their product sprayed around the podium might be a bit galling. They got some free recompense, though, the first race of the 1998 season at Melbourne again saw the Moët lavishly squirted around, compliments of Mr Ecclestone.

Hats Off To The Sun

Pedro Diniz found himself surrounded by flames in his Ligier during the 1996 Argentinian Grand Prix, prompting the superb headline in The Sun: "Diniz In The Oven." Fortunately he escaped unhurt.

Boot Boy

Alexander Wurz wears one red boot and one blue boot when racing.

"Once an accident has started happening you've just got enough time to say 'Sh#t, I'm having a shunt!'" James Hunt

Coulthard: "How do I know you're my real girlfriend?"

Game Racer

Jacques Villeneuve reckons he learns about the intricacies of various circuits by playing them on a Playstation video games console.

Kneesy Does It

Ralph Schumacher and Olivier Panis both found themselves put at the back of the grid for the British Grand Prix in 1998 because neither driver, when asked to take part in a safety check, could escape their cockpits without their knees jamming against the steering column.

Coulthard: "I know I'm kissing you, but how do I know you're my real girlfriend?"

Ecclestone's sales patter needs updating.

Backing Jackie

"Am I worried about losing the image I've created? For me it's not an issue. If you don't go out and try, you ain't going to win anything. Am I going to sit on my arse in front of ITV this season, being no more than an armchair critic? I think I've got more to offer than that. I don't think I'm frightened of not winning." Jackie Stewart explains why he came back into F-1 with his own team.

The Way To Do It

Ricardo Patrese had a magnificent Portuguese Grand Prix in 1991, but was nearly unable to compete at all. Early in qualifying his Williams-Renault blew up, forcing Patrese to turn to the spare car. The spare, however, was set up for team leader Nigel Mansell, who wouldn't allow Patrese in the car until he was satisfied with his own qualifying performance. Which in the end left Patrese just five minutes to get used to the spare (no time to make adjustments, either) and post a qualifying time. He qualified on pole position with his one and only flying lap, and then went on to win the race the next day, too.

You Can't Do That!

Eddie Irvine's Grand Prix debut in a Jordan in 1993 in Japan was not without incident. Irvine had the gall to overtake race leader Ayrton Senna despite having already been lapped. The result was a punch-up between Brazilian and Ulsterman afterwards.

Geoff Brabham

"Racing is 99% boredom and one per cent terror."

How do you spell 'God'?

Tough Job

"You go to a nightclub and you're treated like a VIP. And the police let you off, whatever you've done." Eddie Irvine explains the benefits of being a Ferrari driver in Italy.

Sweet Stuff

Jos Verstappen threatened legal action against a Dutch sweet manufacturer, who was therefore forced to withdraw its latest line of car-shaped candy, originally called "Crashed Verstappens."

Numbers Game

Formula 1 TV watchers in 1996 numbered a mind boggling 50,732,645,052. A lot more people than actually reside on the planet.

Don't Say That

"The only thing that can still go wrong is for the plane to crash on the way home."
Johnny Herbert reflects on a poor time in South America for the Argentine and Brazilian Grand Prix, neither of which he managed to complete.

"No question - Nigel was a whinger;
he was a difficult man.
But he would never give up. On race day he was somebody
you really had to look out for."
Gerhard Berger's assessment of Nigel Mansell.

I'm not really a mechanic!

Foot In Mouth

Mika Hakkinen travelled to the 1998 Argentine Grand Prix with a commanding Championship lead and a dash of over-confidence. He made a remark to the effect of "the other teams will need a miracle to catch us." Hakkinen regretted his words after the race which was won by Michael Schumacher.

You Can't Park There

David Coulthard came in for some stick from team boss Ron Dennis after parking his McLaren during practice and leaving it unguarded. In moved hordes of eager photographers who snapped away at one of the 1998 season's dominant cars. Anyone would think that there were secrets to hide.

Billy Scott

"If a man can f##k and drive race cars, man... I mean, what else is there?"

"Brilliant. Really brilliant. I just remembered who I race for."

Writing On The Wall

Jan Magnussen's final few weeks with the Stewart team in 1998 were not happy ones. In the Argentine GP he managed to qualify dead last on the grid and was forced to call on divine intervention for help: "Some people are praying for rain, but I want a bloody earthquake." Insult was added to injury for Magnussen when he managed to collide with his team-mate Rubens Barrichello on the first lap of the San Marino GP, causing terminal damage to the Stewart number one car.

"Our mirrors are not that good."
Michael Schumacher on how he saw Damon Hill's performance in the Arrows.

Somehow the 100 metre sprint challenge with Linford Christie didn't seem quite fair.

Johnny Herbert - Norman no friends

99 Enough

Jackie Stewart planned to retire after 100 Grand Prix - the landmark coming with the 1973 race in the USA. Stewart wanted to make way for his French understudy, François Cevert. However, in practice for the race, Cevert was killed in a crash. A distressed Stewart called it a day there and then.

Rocketless Rosset

When Ricardo Rosset failed to qualify his Tyrrell for the 1998 Spanish GP by finishing beyond the 107% time margin against the fastest man - it was the first time since the 1997 Australian GP that the grid was not holding the full complement of cars. On the Australian occasion at Melbourne, two drivers had missed out on competing in the race proper - Vicenzo Sospiri and one Ricardo Rosset.

Fake Bearing

One of McLaren's few stumbles in the 1998 season came with the retirement of Mika Hakkinen at the San Marino GP, but it was hardly the driver's fault. The reason for the retirement was because the car had been fitted with a counterfeit gearbox bearing which was unable to cope with the stress of the racing.

"Yes, but my hat's higher."

"I sho

Rich Man's Sport

The Sunday Times top-1000 Rich List featured Mr Formula 1, Bernie Ecclestone, at number six, with an estimated wealth of £1.5 billion.

Fingers crossed

Formula 1 drivers can be a superstitious lot. David Coulthard, for example, always gets into his McLaren from the left hand side, and always right foot first. When driving for the Tyrrell team, Stefano Modena always used to race with one of his driving gloves turned inside out. Former world champion Alan Jones had a lucky pair of underpants that saw him through his career at Williams - although they were held together by a few patches at the end. And Nigel Mansell didn't like anybody else touching his crash helmet before a race.

"Sid, I cannot quit, I have to go on."
Ayrton Senna's last words to
Professor Sid Watkins, Formula 1
surgeon, at Imola in 1994. Senna
crashed and died.

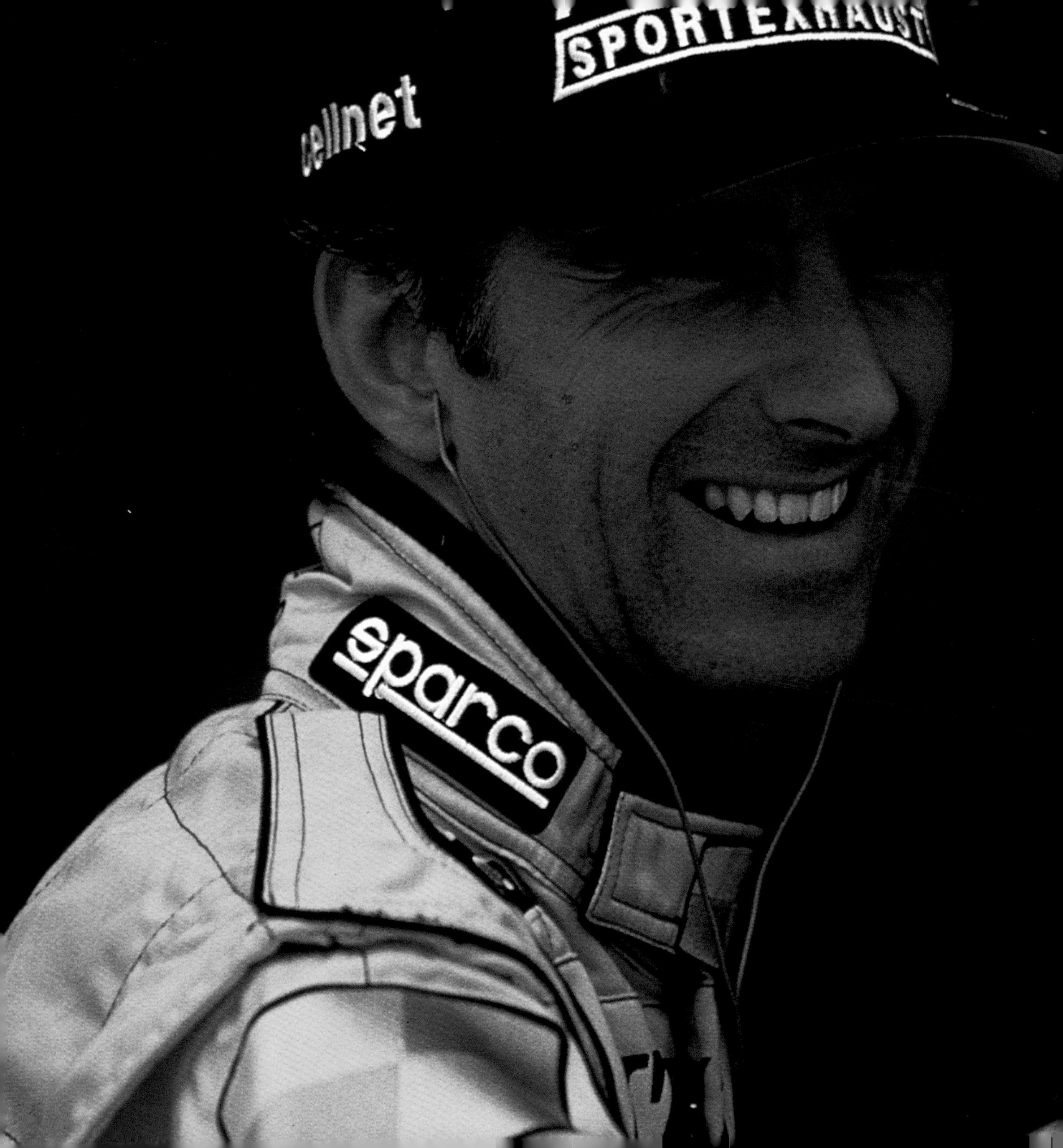
cellnet
sparco

"Coulthard said....this.....?"

"You could just look up at the stars and you just felt you were very, very privileged to be out there driving such a wonderful machine. You weren't doing very much apart from guiding it, but the fact was that it could all go horribly wrong and you'd just be a passenger."
Derek Bell on Le Mans' long Mulsanne straight.

"I get a **buzz** every time I sit in a racing car, every time I start up the engine. If I was earning **£1** a race, I'd still be a racing driver - **just a poor one.**"

Nigel Mansell

Chewy Schuey

Is there no end to the procession of Michael Schumacher spin-off products? One of the latest is Apple flavoured Schumacher bubble gum, sold under the distinctly dodgy tag line of "he's coming out of the pips!"

If Only Everything Was As Reliable...

When both Benetton cars failed to complete the 1998 San Marino GP, it was the first time that both the team's cars had not managed to go the full distance for two years.

Horror For Farina

Ferrari driver Guiseppe Farina was involved in Formula 1's first ever World Championship fatality in 1953. Farina hit and killed a boy crossing the track during the Argentine Grand Prix.

Navigational Trouble

1998 was not a good year for the Arrows team and its driving duo, Pedro Diniz and Mika Salo. The season was perhaps best summed up at Hockenheim for the German GP when the pair left a reception given by sponsor Danka to drive back to their hotel in Waldorf. Using a global positioning satellite navigation system in their car they tapped in Waldorf and headed off, and ended up lost in Frankfurt. There are two Waldorfs in the Hockenheim area.

Still faster than the car...

"Driving a supersonic car is safer than crossing the road."
Andy Green, driver of Thrust, the fastest car on Earth at 763mph.

The Quick And The Dead

In 1970 German driver Jochen Rindt became the first, and thus far only, driver to win the World Championship posthumously. Driving for Lotus, Rindt won in Monaco, Holland, France, Britain and Germany to take the Championship lead, but was then killed in a crash during qualifying for the Italian GP at Monza. The lead he had built up, however, was enough to stay ahead of Ferrari's Jacky Ickx.

Benetton-Playlife wheel changes need serious reevaluation.

"Nigel Mansell is so brave, but such a moaner.
He should have 'He who dares whines'
embroidered on his overalls."

Simon Barnes,
The Times

"When I raced this was called a wheel..."

Canada's Number One

Canada is proud of Jacques Villeneuve - it's official. The 1997 World Champion was awarded Canada's equivalent of the OBE - the Officier de l'Ordre National du Quebec. Jacques must have been doubly chuffed as Celine Dion was also given the award at the same time.

Mercedes Mourning For Le Mans

Mercedes pulled out of motor racing completely in 1955 following the death of more than 80 spectators at the Le Mans 24 Hour race that year. The deaths were a result of Pierre Levegh's Mercedes flying off the track and into the crowd.

Back From The Dead

Niki Lauda made a miraculous return to racing in 1976. The reigning world champion was actually administered the Last Rites after a horrific crash at the Nurburgring in the German GP. Incredibly, Lauda was back in action just three races later, and still led the World Championship come the last race at Fuji. However, torrential rain made conditions for racing abysmal, and Lauda pulled out of the race, leaving James Hunt to take the Championship crown.

Lunch Break

Alfa Romeo entered motor racing in 1924 and quickly made themselves the dominant force. Such was their superiority in the 1925 Belgian Grand Prix that the team's designer, Vittorio Jano, set out a sumptuous lunch in the pit lane and then called his drivers in for them to enjoy a meal while the mechanics polished the cars. Once lunch was over, the drivers went back to the track and continued on their way.

Bring The Car Round James

Road racing in its early days at the turn of the century was very much a pursuit for the rich man - although most cars were actually driven by a chauffeur, because they were the better men behind the wheel.

> ### Gerhard Berger on Senna.
>
> "Ayrton's driving style didn't exist. He didn't have one. When it was time for qualifying, he tailored his driving style to the problems of his car."

Caught Napping

Pedro Diniz knows what it's like to see his car catch fire around him, so he had every right to be concerned at Silverstone when he crashed out of testing in 1998. The engine on Diniz's Arrows blew up at Club Corner but the Brazilian had to wait a full 12 minutes before a marshal arrived with fire extinguisher to help him out. The reason for the marshal's late arrival was a simple one - he had been asleep when the incident occurred. He was sacked afterwards.

Barrichello trying to remember who he drives for. The white car is a good call.

That is the wurz start to a race.

Another Chance Blown

In the 1980s many people wondered whether Nigel Mansell would ever win the world crown. His best chance came in 1986 when, after five wins he was on course to take the title at the last race in Australia, only to see his hopes blown away with his rear tyre. Alain Prost went on to win the title that year, but Mansell finally achieved his dream in 1992.

War Hero

Alfa Romeo's Tipo 158 car was ready to race in 1939 but the Second World War intervened. The new car was hidden in a cheese factory during the German occupation of Italy and was not discovered throughout the duration of the war. It finally made its racing debut immediately after the war ended and dominated the scene for several years.

No Worries

Michael Schumacher produced a breathtaking drive in Hungary in 1998 to win a race that McLaren thought was theirs for the taking. Ferrari technical director Ross Brawn decided to change Schumacher's strategy mid-race: "I got on the radio and told him he had 19 laps to open up the 20-odd seconds he needed for an extra stop," said Brawn. "He took a deep breath and just said 'OK.' That's what he always says..."

Big Ego?

Mika Salo's new house in Helsinki serves as a constant reminder to its owner's trade. Salo has had a mosaic of his crash helmet built into the floor of the indoor swimming pool.

The Monza Gorilla

Vittorio Brambilla, winner of the 1975 Austrian Grand Prix, earned the nickname the Monza Gorilla, due to his style of driving that seemed to lead to more crashes than finishing positions.

Thanks Mum

When it comes to attending the San Marino GP, there is only one team to support - Ferrari. But in the 1998 GP, David Coulthard drew inspiration from a lone Scot waving the St Andrews cross in the midst of a sea of Ferrari red. Coulthard steered his McLaren home five seconds in front of Michael Schumacher's Ferrari, and afterwards paid tribute to his solitary fan: "I couldn't get my mother a ticket and she had to stand over there."

L For Lorenzo

Graham Hill won his only World Championship title in 1962, and but for an unfortunate accident, could have won the title again the following year. Hill missed out narrowly to the Ferrari of John Surtees, but only because Hill was forced out of the final race of the season, the Mexican GP, because his BRM was rammed by the Ferrari of Lorenzo Bandini. Legend has it that Hill sent Bandini a manual on how to drive for Christmas that year.

"I wouldn't go so far as to say that nice guys finish last, but the best **Grand Prix** drivers are driven, motivated, pushy, won't-accept-second-best, immensely competitive people. That is what makes them so good, because they're such bastards."

Frank Williams.

Feline Fever

As a child Niki Lauda had a fear of horses, and he was allergic to cats throughout his life. If only his opponents had known...

Lend Us A Fiver Dear

Colin Chapman founded the Lotus Engineering Company in 1952 with the help of his wife to be, Hazel, who lent him the money.

Mad Michele

Italian driver Michele Albereto kicked off his racing career by driving a car he built himself in his country's Formula Monza series - called by some the "crazy series".

Baldy Boys

Damon Hill captured the World Championship of 1996 at the Japanese GP at Suzuka. Hill celebrated by taking to the karaoke machine at Suzuka's Log Cabin, backed by the now shaven-headed trio of Jacques Villeneuve, David Coulthard and Mika Salo.

"Do you come here often?"   "Unfortunately because of you, yes."

Turn The Wheel!

David Coulthard began to make a name for himself in F1 circles during his first full season in a Williams in 1995. He won his first GP that year at Portugal, but suffered a couple of near misses as well. The first was at the British GP which he led before having to take a stop-go penalty, but it was at Australia that he caused his own downfall. Leading comfortably, Coulthard entered the pit straight for a routine stop but failed to take the corner - his Williams simply ploughed nose first into the pit lane wall.

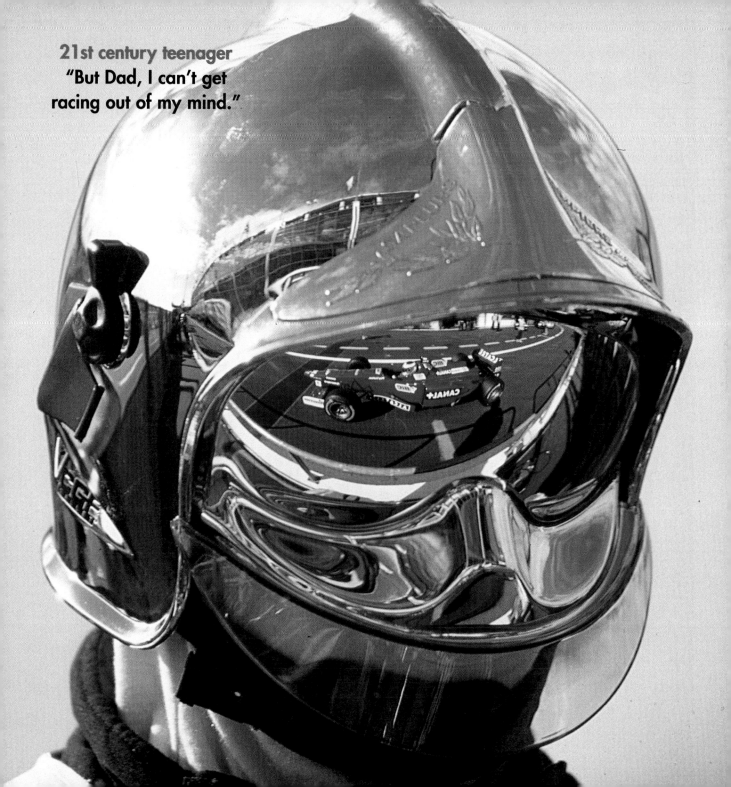

21st century teenager
"But Dad, I can't get racing out of my mind."

"**DC** understands the team player bit because he is intelligent and a real person. The hard thing, for people of his ilk, is to remain a great driver. You don't have to be thick to drive quickly in **F1** - **but it helps.**"
F1 Racing magazine's Peter Windsor tells it how it is.

Reader's break. Enjoy!

The Aim Is To Cross the Finish Line

Andrea de Cesaris drove for Brabham in 1987 but did not manage to finish one race. However, he still managed to claim third place in the Belgian GP, despite the fact that he had pulled off the race track because his car had run out of fuel.

Close Call

English driver Peter Gethin holds the distinction of winning the closest ever Grand Prix. It came in 1971 in Austria, with Gethin driving his first race for BRM having been dumped by McLaren because of poor results. Gethin pushed his car to the front of a five vehicle pack to edge home in front of Ronnie Peterson's March by a mere 0.01 seconds. Howden Ganley came fifth in the race and was still only 0.61 seconds behind the winner. It was Gethin's only ever Grand Prix victory.

Looking Forward To Retirement?

Argentine legend Juan Manuel Fangio had an eventful last season of driving before he retired. He ran his own Maserati in a couple of Grand Prix, competed in the Indy 500 for the first time, and even managed to get himself kidnapped when he was in Cuba for a sports car race.

"Today, I am testing ze new Schumacher ice cream. Sadly, it does not taste as good as me."

In The Hunt

British ace James Hunt earned the nickname Hunt The Shunt because of his tendency to crash a lot, although the habit actually got him into the F1 scene a little quicker than anticipated. Hunt was part of the Hesketh team who planned a season of Formula 2 racing to gain experience, but Hunt managed to destroy the car, so the team decided to enter into F1 using a chassis provided by March. Hunt steered the car into the points in just his second F1 race.

Fast Start

Mike Hawthorn entered the racing world in style. Hawthorn competed in three races in an event at Goodwood - won the first, then beat Fangio in the second to win that as well, and finally was narrowly beaten by Argentine ace Jose Gonzalez. People took notice of the young Hawthorn, especially given the fact that the event was his racing debut in a single seater car.

Trust The French

Murray Walker is forever reminding us about the Bridgestone - Goodyear tyre war in F1, but obviously French watchers of Formula 1 racing don't hear Murray's commentary because one of the reasons Michelin has for not entering the F1 tyre business is because 60% of the people polled in France think Michelin are already involved in the pit lane.

Dancing For Johnny

Since signing for the Sauber team in 1996, British driver Johnny Herbert has become something of a celebrity in Switzerland and is a regular on Swiss television shows including, bizarrely, with his own dance troupe.

"Honestly, Doc, I woke up this morning and my right ear had given birth to a finger."

Driven To Politics

Carlos Reutemann quit Formula 1 in 1982 and turned his attention to politics, rising to the position of senator in his home country of Argentina.

"**Motor racing's** less of a sport these days, more a commercial break doing 150mph." **Peter Dunne,** Independent on Sunday. "I'm not suicidal or anything, but I have fun when I'm on the **edge.**"
Jacques Villeneuve.

Boobs 4, Balls 2.

"No comment."

Ring Rage

Jackie Stewart won the 1968 German GP at the infamous Nurburgring and counts it as one of the highlights of his career. "Had I not won a Grand Prix at the Nurburgring, there would have been something missing from my career - but wasn't it a ridiculous place? Leaping from one bump to another, 187 corners or whatever it was! The number of times I thanked God when I finished a lap. I can't remember doing one more balls-out lap of the 'Ring than I needed to. It gave you amazing satisfaction, but anyone who says he loved it is either a liar or wasn't going fast enough. I like that place best when I'm sitting by a log fire on a winter's night. Clear in my mind are all the braking distances and gear changes, and that's surely the only way I've ever lapped it without a mistake."

Death By Politeness

Motor racing's first fatality occurred in 1898 during a Paris-Nice race. Monsieur de Montariol politely pulled aside to wave through the quicker car of the Marquis de Montaignac. The Marquis, however, took his hands off the steering tiller to wave thanks, but swerved and actually ran the car of M. de Montariol off the road. It overturned, and although M. de Montariol was thrown clear, his mechanic died from his injuries. The Marquis turned to watch the crash and his car also overturned, ultimately killing the driver.

Computer Error

Nigel Mansell suffered some cruel blows in his F1 career, but one of the worst came in the 1991 Canadian GP as Mansell entered the final lap in first place, more than a minute ahead of Nelson Piquet's Benetton. Less then a mile from the finish, Mansell's Williams suffered a blip in its gear change software, and the car's revs dropped and the engine died. Piquet was told by his pit crew to push on, which he did, and he won the race. The fault in Mansell's car took a mere five minutes to locate and fix to ensure it would never happen again. Too late, though...

Born To Be Wild

French driver Patrick Depailler was of the playboy breed, but team boss Ken Tyrrell managed to keep a close rein on his rising star. It was a shame that Tyrrell didn't pass on some handling advice when Depailler moved on to Ligier. Tyrrell had a clause in Depailler's contract forbidding him playing with "dangerous toys" - Ligier did not. Said Depailler: "I waited five years to go hang-gliding when I was with Tyrrell, and I started it the week after I left."

Sadly, Depailler's skills in the air were not in the same class as when he was behind the wheel. Sure enough, he crashed and suffered serious leg injuries which kept him out of motor racing for six months.

Ski Racer

Before trying his luck at racing, Patrick Tambay was actually on the verge of the French national ski team.

"Sorry, I don't allow smoking in my car."

"Are you trying to f####### kill me?"

Michael Schumacher confronts David Coulthard after they collided in the rain at the Belgian GP in 1998.

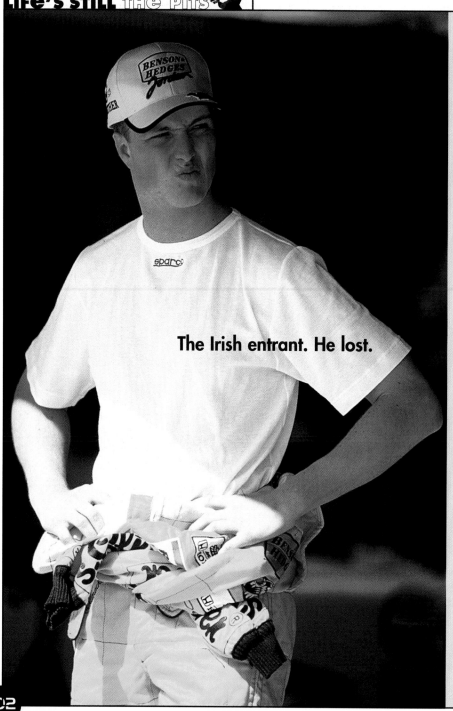

The Irish entrant. He lost.

We are immortal

Ever wondered where Silverstone got the names for its now famous corners? Some came from nearby landmarks such as Stowe School, but several came from the names of the serving RAC competition committee when the circuit was formed.

Fast Fuel

A new mix of fuel induced high performance in F1 in 1983 - the petrol was subsequently found to be rocket fuel.

Champion Swimmer

Alberto Ascari, a world champion with Ferrari in 1952 and 1953, was an Italian folk hero. He also holds a distinguished place in the mystique of the Monaco Grand Prix because in 1955, when challenging for the lead, Ascari lost control in a chicane, and his Lancia hurtled through the straw bales and into the Monaco harbour. Ascari sank with the car, then surfaced with injuries no more serious than a broken nose.

Spooky

The death of Italian legend Alberto Ascari was a strange one. Just weeks after cheating death by driving his car into the Monaco harbour, he travelled to Monza to watch his friend Eugenio Castellotti test a new Ferrari, and decided to have a few laps himself. He borrowed Castellotti's helmet and took the Ferrari out, only to crash fatally on his third lap. Ascari's father Alberto was also a driver - he died in a crash in the French GP in 1925. When they crashed fatally, both were 36 years old. In addition, both died while wearing someone else's crash helmet, and both had escaped a bad accident unscathed just weeks before their deaths. Coincidence?

Lights Out

The 1930 Mille Miglia race was a battle between the Alfa Romeo drivers, Nuvolari and Varz. Driving in the dark of the morning of the second day, Varz, some three minutes ahead of Nuvolari on the road but behind on aggregate time, spotted the headlights of his rival's car behind him. Minutes later, the lights disappeared, and Varz thought the race was won because Nuvolari had been forced to retire. So it came as a bit of a surprise just 30 miles from the finish when Nuvolari's car tooted its horn, flashed its headlights and sped past a startled Varz. Nuvolari had driven all the way down the mountain stretch of the race in the dark, without lights.

"The moments of joy in our sport are very intense, but very short. And they have to be overlaid very quickly by normal work if you want to continue to be successful."
Ayrton Senna

Mirrors just
don't do justice.

Harsh Words

After Ricardo Rosset rammed Jacques Villeneuve during practice for the 1998 Monaco GP, the Canadian World Champion was less then complimentary about the skills of Rosset in the Tyrrell. "There are drivers who just should not be part of Grand Prix racing and he is one of them. He is a liability, a danger. Whenever you get close to him you have to think: 'What will he do now?'"

Rosset bought his way into the Tyrrell team by paying £3 million for the privilege of racing one of their cars.

A Long And Fruitless Career

Andrea de Cesaris enjoyed a long Formula 1 career, some 208 races. It is also the record number of Grand Prix starts made by a driver without scoring a win.

Moving Troubles

Jackie Stewart and his son Paul decided to move their Stewart-Ford racing team to Milton Keynes in 1998 - no easy thing to carry out. Said Jackie: "You know how stressful it is to move house, so you can imagine what it's like moving a racing team."

"I don't remember... I can't honestly say... I don't know exactly... I can't remember the exact date... I don't honestly remember..." Damon Hill gives evidence at the inquest into Ayrton Senna's death.

"Can you trust this man to run a public company?"

Business Age magazine headline on an article about Bernie Ecclestone's bid to float Formula 1 racing on the stock market.

Bad Times

The four year period of 1966 to 1969 was a grim time for Formula 1. Some 34 drivers were killed during this time, an alarming rate of deaths. It could have been more - Jackie Stewart was rescued from his BRM which had ended up in a ditch after leaving the track in the 1966 Belgian GP. Soaked in petrol, Stewart was unable to get out of the car without the timely help of team-mate Graham Hill and Bob Bondurant, who had both crashed in the same incident as Stewart.

It's Called Racing

Michael Schumacher took exception to Damon Hill's attempt to defend his track position during the 1998 Canadian GP, but the Daily Telegraph columnist, Robert Hardman, set Scumacher straight: "The incident looked like what it was - a fierce tussle for second place. It was what traditionalists call "racing", although we see so little actual "racing" these days that Schumacher may simply have forgotten what it is."

Sponsorship versus health debate.

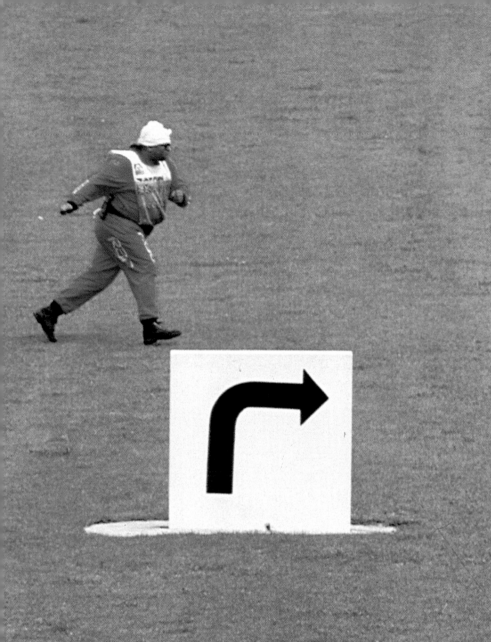

"There's a woolly hat on the track."

"There's a twat
on the track."

Soft Walls

American Indy Racing began testing new safety measures during the 1998 season, unveiling a system of padding the concrete walls around the track to cushion impact blows.

"Ayrton has a small problem. He thinks he can't kill himself because he believes in God, and I think that's very dangerous for the other drivers." Alain Prost

Learn To Drive

Swansea's Institute of Higher Education is now offering a degree in motor racing - or rather "motorsport engineering and design" to give it its proper title.

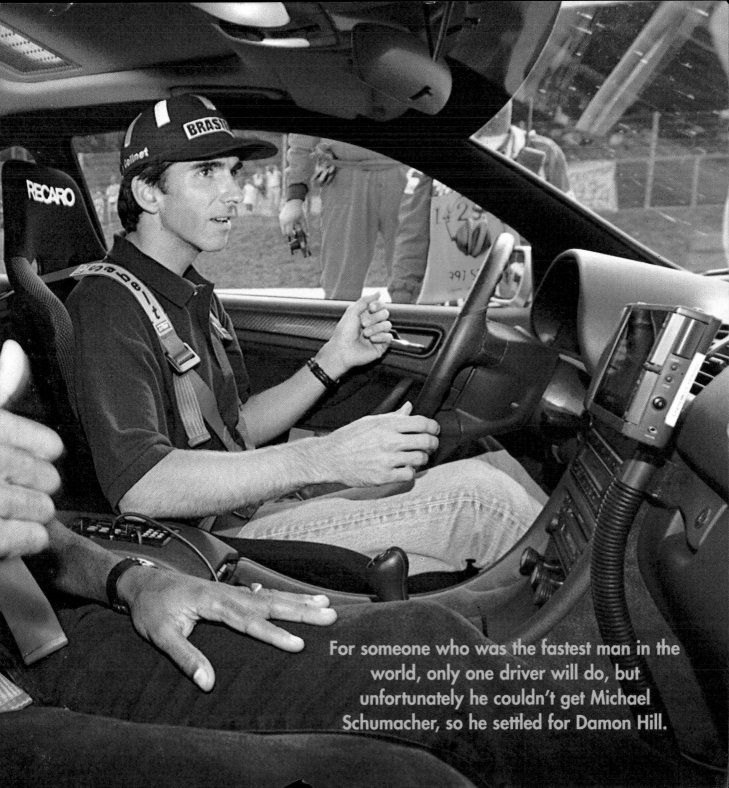

For someone who was the fastest man in the world, only one driver will do, but unfortunately he couldn't get Michael Schumacher, so he settled for Damon Hill.

IF YOU ENJOYED THIS BOOK, WHAT ABOUT THESE!

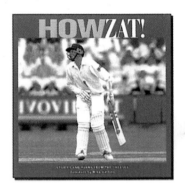

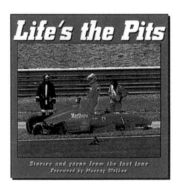
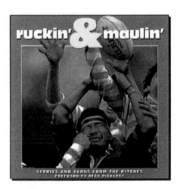

All these books are available at your local bookshop or can be ordered direct from the publisher.
Just list the titles you require and give your name address, including postcode.
Prices and availability are subject to change without notice.

Please send to Chameleon Cash Sales, 76 Dean Street, London W1V 5HA, a cheque or postal order for £7.99 and add the following for postage and packaging:
UK - £1.00 For the first book, 50p for the second and 30p for the third and for each additional book up to a maximum of £3.00.
OVERSEAS - (including Eire) £2.00 For the first book, £1.00 for the second and 50p for each additional book up to a maximum of £3.00.